This is the Truth:

I'm not really old enough to be anybody's Grandmother

Written by Barbara Defago
Illustrated by Marcela González

Copyright @ 2014 by Barbara Defago
All rights reserved
ISBN:1497559693

This is a work of creative non-fiction. All incidents described and attendant advice is based on real-life observations and experiences which are colored by the author's imagination and dark sense of humor. Having said that, she takes no responsibility for how your grandchildren turn out or any consequences you may suffer as a result of following the suggestions contained herein.

We may have chosen to become mothers, but somebody else had the nerve to make us grandmothers.

If you're holding this book, it's dedicated to you. If you recognize yourself on these pages, you might want to ponder that for a while.

HI THERE

If you could see me right now, you'd know that I'm an honest down-to-earth, no-nonsense kind of gal. I'm not sure I like that word—gal—but I'm going to leave it here for the time being. Anyway, it's important that you know something about me in order to truly engage with the meaningful information to follow. I gave birth when I was a mere child myself and said offspring has followed suit. So that makes me—hold on to your hat—a grandmother. I know, it's hard for all of us to believe (you'd have to see me to know that's true), but it is a reality.

So, being a person who is always seeking to improve herself, I have reflected on this life passage, if you will—perhaps like a dog with a bone, but that's my way. I want to share it all with you just because I like you. Nobody really ever gave me any good advice, so now it's my turn. Everything you are about to read has come from my experiences as a woman, which includes all of those "roles" such as personal valet and chauffeur as well as my observations and conclusions as a teacher and therapist who got to know a lot of really nice screwed-up people.

I'd like to give a nod to the self-help industry whose mission it is to find more and more stuff for us to work on; self-awareness is key they say. Thanks also to the global community for making it okay for me to hug strangers and bare my soul.
It is my hope that the reader (you) will come away with the comforting knowledge that she is not alone on this awe-filled journey, which as we all know, is way more valuable than the destination. It would be good as well if you are able to add a few new "tools" to your grandmotherly repertoire.

How to use this book: Pick it up, put it down, skip around if you like or read it from start to finish while you fry your eggs. I like to think of it as an "interaction" between you and me.

It has no end because you'll most likely be tempted to add to it as inspirations strike you. Feel free. I wrote it down as it came to me, not in order of importance. You can be the judge of that. Along the way, I hope my reminders to "see" other sections are helpful.

Also, a companion notebook of your choosing would be handy to record your ramblings as this will help you to refine your grand parenting. Let's get started.

CONTENTS

BE VERY CLEAR THAT THIS LITTLE SPROUT IS YOUR REASON FOR LIVING
TELL YOUR SASSY ONE THAT YOU LOVE HIM/HER OFTEN AND MAKE SURE HE/SHE RECIPROCATES
BE AVAILABLE, ACCOMODATING AND MOST IMPORTANTLY—ADVENTUROUS
CREATE THOSE MEMORIES
THERE'S NO "GRACEFUL" IN OLD, SO DON'T BE IT
GET WITH THE PROGRAM: BE COMPETITIVE
CORNER THE MARKET ON THE BEST TOYS
READ EVERYTHING YOU CAN ABOUT PARENTING SO YOU CAN DO A BETTER JOB THIS TIME AROUND
SETTING UP THE ENVIRONMENT
LIKE THE ENVIRONMENT, BUT ON A DEEPER LEVEL
BE EQUIPPED
SHOW ONE EMOTION—HAPPY—AND NEVER EVER SWEAR
MAINTAIN YOUR OPTIMUM FITNESS LEVEL
NUTRITION AND MEDICAL ISSUES (WITH A NOTE ABOUT POTTY-TRAINING)
ALWAYS BE PRESENT
WATCH TV
IT'S A BOY...OR IS IT A GIRL?
SLEEP
TIME
GUNS AND VIOLENCE
THE IMPORTANCE OF KEEPING THEM BUSY
MODELING CAREERS AND OTHER LIMELIGHT
DISCIPLINE—IF IT'S EVER REQUIRED
NOTES TO SELF

BE VERY CLEAR THAT THIS LITTLE SPROUT IS YOUR REASON FOR LIVING

Remember when you told the issue from your loins to "knock it off" because you "gave him/her life"? Well this endearing grandmotherly way is kind of like that except in a reversed sort of manner. Tell your member of this new generation that he/she is your raison d'etre. Without him/her your life would have nada meaning. Before he/she came on the scene, you were just wandering around gazing vacantly into the horizon, waiting. Oh, I know, you might be thinking that being the sole purpose for another person's existence is a huge responsibility, but, hey, that's what life is—a lot of heavy burdens. So why not start learning that at an early age, huh? This will lay the seeds for a close relationship down the line. When you are very ancient your nearly grown-up cuddler will be giving you pedicures in the old folks' home instead of spending his/her time on silly pursuits like dating and bar-hopping.

Take up your notebook and reflect on all the future positive outcomes of keeping junior in line with this reminder. A few pages might be required.

TELL YOUR SASSY ONE HOW MUCH YOU LOVE HIM/HER OFTEN AND MAKE SURE HE/SHE RECIPROCATES

This is a really important one because children have very short memories, with the exception of the time you abandoned him/her on a ski hill, which will be trotted out on a regular basis until you die. So all the more reason to start early and refer to yourself in the third person because this will make you realize that first person "I" no longer exists.

Tell him/her "Grandma" (or whatever you want to be called and that issue will be addressed later) "loves you SO much".

Then ask "Do you love Grandma?" because as everyone understands, it's a real bummer to tell someone you love them and be greeted with a blank stare. In other contexts it's downright humiliating; remember those guys forty years ago who either looked shell-shocked at your stupid confession or said something lame like "Love ya too"? You know the ones. So now at this stage in your life, don't be shy about asking directly and demanding sincerity. In addition, be adamant that your version of "grandma" is the first word in his/her vocabulary. Oh yeah, and don't forget to reward compliance with treats (cookies are good); thinking about how you trained your pooch will help get you on track.

BE AVAILABLE, ACCOMODATING AND MOST IMPORTANTLY—ADVENTUROUS

Always be available to spend time with the wee one because his/her parents need a lot of breaks. It doesn't matter what you may have planned for Tuesday, when the request to take him/her comes at 10pm on Monday, claim to have nothing else to do and express anticipatory glee to partake in kiddy fun times. You could say this is a form of lying. But what the heck, it will ramp up your Granny-points (See previous section in reference to "I").

Be accommodating. This goes hand in hand with being available, but a little trickier as it involves a certain degree of juggling, especially as the little sweetheart gets older. In terms of this one, it's good to have a full tank of gas and a daytimer (an old-style one will do), because you may have multiple pickups and deliveries to sort out. It can get pretty complicated, but never say you can't handle it. Keep your vision of super-granny ever-present in your mind. If you do happen to screw up the odd time and the kidlet is left on the curb for a while, you must swear him/her to secrecy. Better yet, try reframing it as a positive learning experience. Say something like "Grandma was a little (if less than two hours) late, but wasn't that fun and let's talk about what you learned". Be sure to replace any negative statements he/she may offer through his/her tears with happy thoughts. Oh yes, along with the gas and daytimer, get yourself a cell-phone.

Are you adventurous by nature? Take this quiz to find out.

- Are you comfortable falling down on ice?
- Do you believe that hair needs to be its natural colour?
- Do you own hiking boots that have been worn?
- Do you currently ride your bike into town and enjoy every minute of it?
- Do you like to be surrounded by brightly coloured plastic balls and mice that jump out of the walls and sing songs?
- Are you willing to play in the dirt and not complain about it wrecking your manicure?
- Do you consider Halloween an occasion for decorating your house inside and out?

Sorry for these questions which clearly indicate my own take on being adventurous. I'm sure you have your personal ad-scale to determine whether you're a risk taker or a tad on the cautious side. The point here is to develop awareness of the issues you need to address; only then can you fully get in the groove from babyhood to adolescence by becoming a cool participant with that new little someone in your life. Starting now.

Pick up your notebook to reflect on your adventurous self. Don't worry about how many pages you use.

CREATE THOSE MEMORIES

Document, document, document—in a good way. Have the camera always at the ready to capture those special smiles and cute antics. Some might count this as a number one grandmother rule. Don't be caught without pictures of your chubby cherub. Make sure, too, that you are visible in many of these moments to share. Images of himself/herself hugging and kissing granny always please family, friends, in laws and strangers in the check-out line as well. Diligent documentation (visual and written) provides a record for future enjoyment. It's a sort of "this is your life and aren't you really glad that I got it all down as proof" for your pipsqueak. Never underestimate the power of the past. If you live long enough to witness his/her first romance, sit yourself down between the love birds with your visual retrospective in hand. This is a great ice-breaker...and those artful shots of your two year old superkid wearing nothing but a pair of sunglasses are sure to captivate his/her prospective life partner.

A helpful tip: Have your charming charge recite each and every oh-so-fun time he/she has had with you. This is another form of documentation as it burns it into his/her little brain for later retrieval at family dinners and the like. The 'other' grandmother will be sure to take note. Don't worry if he/she doesn't get it right the first time. Repetition is a key element of learning to remember, so go over it with your reason for being as many times as it takes and don't leave out any details.

THERE'S NO "GRACEFUL" IN OLD, SO DON'T BE IT

We all know that getting old sucks; it must be avoided. Out of the gate, you have to stand out as a grandmamma. You simply have to establish your place in the line, right up front by looking your best (which means young). This takes considerable effort, but it's definitely worth it as it will pay off for you in the long run and your rugrat will be on his/her way to negotiating those curve balls that life sends him/her because he/she will understand the value of appearance. Here are some makeover suggestions to consider. Ditch the elasticized polyester, unless it's of the stylin' variety that has recently come back, and trade in the arch supports. If you're looking for jeans, avoid the "mom" variety that sit high up above your little pot belly. Remember, no one should look at you and see the 80's which, by the way, we need to forget. Spruce up your do with a cut and color; ocean shades are popular these days. Regarding ink (tattoos): go for classic images like butterflies or paisley patterns and choose a spot on your body that is the least likely to fall prey to gravity and distort the artwork—perhaps the ankle. Facial piercings should be discrete; I suggest no more than eight in the ears and a single stud in the nose; stay away from your belly. Pick up some magazines for the latest and the hottest trends in clothing, shoes and accessories. The higher the heels, the better; developing the calves is a side benefit (See MAINTAIN YOUR OPTIMUM LEVEL OF FITNESS). You'll know you're groovy when at least one person expresses incredulity at the fact that you are indeed a grandmother. To this, simply smile and say something cute like "Well, I was a teen mum and my child followed in my footsteps" (a form of role-modeling).

Start a "To-Do" list in your notebook. To begin, sit quietly for a few minutes and think about who you really are and how to express that on the outside. Are you a diva or maybe a vixen? Perhaps you are drawn to punk-rock or the laid-back tunes of the 70's (they were okay). We're all unique, so go for it. There's nothing standing in your way to creating a look that screams "I am me"! Once again, use as much space as you need; I'd suggest at least 10 items. While you're at it, how about adding a little pizzazz to your persona by adopting a non-traditional name for yourself? It could be something like "Gigi" which clearly represents young and hip as opposed to old and boring.

For a moment, let's imagine that you've got the look going. That's a really good first step, but fine-tuning the inner you can be a bit more challenging. How often do we hear

"Believe in yourself" or "I'm wonderful just the way I am" or (and this is the cruel one) "I love my wrinkles"?

Get out your notebook and make a list of popular self-affirming statements that, if you were honest, have scored at least a 5/10 on the "I feel like throwing up" scale. Start with 5's and end with 10's to make it easier on yourself. Your notebook is waiting.

Once again, sit quietly and slowly read over your list. You need to embrace each and every item. By that, I mean breathe them in and make them a part of who you are. Please don't ask me for specifics on how to do this, just repeat repeat repeat like a mantra. Eventually the inside will be matching that fantastic outer you whether you be diva, vixen or whatever. So great!!

Whew—quite a lot to digest, I know, but perseverance will find you on the path to becoming a bitchin´ grandee. Have patience and realize you're bound to run into some forks in the road. Be kind to yourself.

GET WITH THE PROGRAM: BE COMPETITIVE

Everyone knows that life is a competition. Science has told us about survival of the fittest, after all. We vie for grades, jobs, awards and of course—love. Grannyhood is a perfect opportunity to share your superlativeness with the world because although it's fabuloso to know that you're at the head of the pack, it's almost inconsequential unless others know it too. Here's where social media comes in. I know, I know—we're just not very adept at learning this new tool for disseminating important information. But learn we must. Get yourself on Myfacebook and Twitterbug and all the other places to spread your word out there. Make sure you have a lot of "friends" and put up pictures EVERY DAY of your cutiepie. It helps to add a brief commentary to each one; maybe something like "Here he/she is looking so very sweet in the new parka grandma (refer to yourself in the third person) bought him/her". It's actually quite a lot of fun when people "comment" on them. Most of the time they say things like "AWWWWW" or "SOOOOO PRECIOUS" or "YOU'RE ONE LUCKY GRANDMA!!!!!" to express their true feelings. The really neat ones come in the form of "YOU'RE THE BEST". You, yes, you. So fine tune those grey cells and start cutting, pasting and posting. It's all about marketing, they say.

While you're at it, collect a few old-fashioned bumper stickers that tell the world about how much you enjoy your status. Something like "I heart my grandchildren" would be good. Get creative and make your own sticker that is unique to you. I recommend avoiding anything slightly snarky or self-centred like "I'm spending my kids' inheritance" as that casts doubt on your stellar qualities as a grandmother. Ready set go...there's no time like the present to start the competition.

You could think of this as your portfolio or your resume. Make a list of one thing to do each day to start this process. Perhaps begin with "open a Myfacebook account" and don't forget to include possible sticker sayings. It's all up to you. Use a separate piece of paper for this one to keep on your desk in front of your computer.

CORNER THE MARKET ON THE BEST TOYS

Easy-peasy. The trick is to start early. At least six months before a birthday, holiday or any meaningful milestone in your mini one's life (like that first tooth for example), get out there and shop, shop, shop! Themes are good. You know—cars/trains for the little guys and fake nails/hair accessories for the tiny girlies. Don't just buy one piece of the collection, however. Get the train and ALL the tracks, stations, houses, trees and people that go along with it. Battery operated gizmos are good too in this electronic age; they make a lot of noise and stimulate brains. Buy in duplicate so that the parents of your sweetie will be reminded of all the stuff you get for him/her. Tripping over it in the middle of the night and activating sounds that wake the babe won't bother them, because, as you know, good parents never complain or swear.

If you are living on a meager pension, don't worry. I frequently run across some great items parked at the side of the road and second-hand stores are bursting with joyfulness when it comes to kids' toys. This is due to the little-understood fact that tots abuse them, cast them aside after fifteen minutes and fickly move on, thus prompting parents to load them (the toys, not the kids) into their newly-purchased van and deposit yesterday's treasures outside the nearest thrift shop. If you decide to go this route, just be cautious and examine the item for broken bits and body fluids and treat accordingly.

Oh yeah, I almost forgot to tell you that it's crucial to let the others know that you got the cool goods well in advance of the occasion. This prevents them from raining on your parade, so to speak. Best toys equal best grandmothers, after all.

READ EVERYTHING YOU CAN ABOUT PARENTING SO YOU CAN DO A BETTER JOB THIS TIME AROUND

Don't get me wrong. This is not to say that you didn't do a bang-up job the first time around. Everybody knows that. I mean, just take a look at your beautiful, intelligent multi-talented, star-quality offspring. And he/she owes all of that to you, as ungrateful as he/she might be. His/her therapist is totally convinced of that, I might add. But there's always room for improvement on this journey of life and there's a lot of good stuff out there written by true experts. I do recommend, however, staying away from reading anything that presents contradictory views. Let's face it, you know best.

A quick scan of the parenting literature will tell you that being a role model is hot right now. No longer is it just fine to admonish wee people with "Do as I say, not as I do". I'm not sure why that has gone out of fashion, but trust me, it has. Perhaps this paradigmatic shift is the result of new research on child behaviour. It's been discovered that ankle-biters fresh out are watching you all the time. Talk about pressure, huh? There are actually phone numbers available for kids to bust you. With that in mind there are lots of things to NOT do in front of them. A partial list might include the obvious such as talking on the phone while your dearest darling is on the teeter-totter (see ALWAYS BE PRESENT), screaming at your husband even when he deserves it (See SHOW ONE EMOTION—HAPPY—AND NEVER EVER SWEAR) or getting wasted at his/her birthday shindig. You get it; now go to your notebook and add to this list. When you're done, read it over and pick one to work on. Think baby steps. Tomorrow is another day and another way to be the best. Use as much paper as you need.

Later, when you're all sitting around watching his/her adorable little self, be sure to connect all the positive behaviours to none other than vous. Here's an example: "Will you look at that! (Insert child's name here) is sharing his/her toy so nicely. When I took him/her to the Science Centre today, there was a fabulous interactive learning booth and I said to (insert child's name here) blah, blah, blah........." Almost any situation can be used to illustrate your commitment to teaching your precious petunia good conduct/values/morals and reminding his/her parents of your invaluable wisdom.

SETTING UP THE ENVIRONMENT

I'll touch on some basics of three environments, just so you get the gist.

In the home: It is a must right from the get-go to renovate your house. Add on a few rooms or knock down a wall if need be, to create a space that is safe and welcoming. Remove all forms of decoration and suspend the knick-knacks from the ceiling. Remember that almost everything in your house is a potential choking hazard, regardless of size.

Make it impossible for your bundle of joy to open any cupboards. You can buy special latches that prevent said bundles from getting their grimy hands on toxic materials. Note to the reader: Be sure to practice opening/closing so you can comfortably access necessary toxins. Take inventory of your home with "kid-friendly" at the forefront of your mind in order to protect everyone concerned. This may result in removal of all lighter pieces of furniture (such as dining chairs) to minimize falling opportunities when he/she is finding his/her sea legs. Learn to eat standing up. Oh, and don't forgot those little scatter mats you've got lying around as they present a slipping opportunity. If you have a gas fireplace, never turn it on. Get in the habit of viewing it as a nice piece of cold glass on the wall. Buy yourself a few hand sanitizer stations (like the ones they have in hospitals); one in every room is preferable. You should never be complacent about germs.

If you are brave and leave some of your stuff out, just rethink your priorities with the knowledge that designer coffee tables and hand-knotted silk rugs are appropriate places for scratchy toys and gooey substances.

In the car: There's a lot to learn about this one. Sadly, the old days when we made a quick run to the store with the kid in our lap, have gone. Now we are required to strap them in until they are seventeen or 120 pounds (whichever comes first). Not only that, but they have to be in the back seat because now we have airbags that could kill them. I'm not finished yet. Facing backwards or forwards? Acquaint yourself with the finer details, please. Dreaming of a sportscar? Nix on that, Nellie. Just like you and your house, a car makeover/update is in order. You're going to need four doors, adequate cargo space for the equipment that you require (which will be addressed in an upcoming section) and ample head room for moving him/her in and out with minimal cranial trauma.

If you happen to be a country girl who drives a pick-up, a whole other set of rules apply. First off, don't chuck those babes in the open box of the truck; leave that space for your pit bull to enjoy. A motorcycle gal? Don't even go there, Honey.

In the world at large: We know the world is a very dangerous place, but now that we are grandmothers it is our duty to be ever-vigilant. Keep your eyes peeled on him/her at all times or he/she may die. I recently heard about a woman who allowed her 27 year old son to ride the subway unsupervised. That's just plain dumb, I say. Be aware that there are hazards at every turn. Lots of cars, buses, people of questionable motives and dirt anxiously waiting to be consumed. You might consider investing in a leash as this is a great piece of equipment for animal lovers that works for kids too.

Additional thoughts: I'm sure you've heard of "helicopter moms". Some apropos metaphors for grandmothers include "magnifying glass grammas" who concentrate on in-depth inspection and removal of harmful substances, potential pitfalls and crusty things on the face; and then there are "vacuum g-mas" who suck up things in the environment of home, car and the world at large in order to protect their loved littles while exposing themselves to harm (but that's okay).

BEWARE: You do not want to turn into a "venus fly trap grandma". It's a slippery slope. Here are some of the early warning signs and symptoms:
- A slight quivering around the mouth at the mere mention of your angel
  - Tingling of the fingers as he/she approaches
  - Hypnotic staring into his/her orbits

•Incessant licking of the lips sometimes accompanied by a staccato-like biting of the air

If you experience one or more of the above, take yourself off to Mexico for a long time.

LIKE THE ENVIRONMENT, BUT ON A DEEPER LEVEL

Now that you've got the physical space tickety-boo, it's time to look at some other aspects of the environment. What is important for you to provide for that squirmy miss/master? You want to be seen as fun, yes. But beyond that, learning opportunities are everywhere and you must take advantage of them. Related to the previous section on environmental spaces, here are some suggestions: Wherever you find yourself with him/her whether it's the home, car, or world at large, always capitalize on those teachable moments.

Sing all the time even if you've experienced psychological damage at the hands of your child who took enjoyment in criticizing your lack of melodic competence. It's good for your grandchild. Dance even when you are driving as this is an indicator of your natural spontaneity as well as a learning opp that no one will ever understand, but it's real. Get down with your kiddy. Be in his/her face at all times. Play with the cars, make zoom-zoom noises and pretend the doll is a baby. Whatever it takes. Be a child again, no matter how foreign that seems. He/she will remember these times and thank you for them.

Invest in some good quality flashcards for use when your toddie is in his/her highchair. This will dramatically increase his/her language proficiency and will be something remarkable to talk about for years to come. When he/she enters the school system his/her kindergarten teacher will be amazed that he/she has attained a grade three reading level at age 5 and this will all be due to your outstanding skills as a grandmother.

Arrange play-dates with other folks' badly behaved children. This is how himself/herself will learn about conflict resolution, sharing and all kinds of other things related to socializing and important life skills. When those little dears bonk him/her over the head with a 3-pound truck it's sure to have a significant impact.

Speaking of the aforementioned little dears, let's talk candidly. Other people's children are basically a pain. But, a little tolerance goes a long way. Expose your perfect one to the "other" as it will become obvious to all that he/she is, in every possible arena, head-and-shoulders above them. You can also use these creatures as negative examples which helps to develop your angel's healthy sense of self-esteem.

This might be a good opportunity to drag out your notebook in order to make a list of all the ways in which your numero uno is just that.

BE EQUIPPED

Unless you want to be loading up the contents of your charmer's parents' house every time he/she comes for a few hours or a week, deck out your own domicile with baby goods, then toddler stuff and pre-school paraphernalia. Don't get too attached to any of it though, because in the blink of an eye it will be up for sale (going cheap) or in storage awaiting the arrival of little sis/bro. Aside from toys, here are some things you will need to survive:

- Diapers (a must)
- Something for him/her to catch a few winks in
- A secure chair that is high up
- A contraption to take him/her for a tour of the neighbourhood (a good chance to share pics)
- A thing to bounce around in
- A thing to sit in that apparently exercises mind and body
- A mat for when he/she is on his/her tummy (use this at least twice a day to develop neck muscles)
- A thing to push around (similar to those used by old people in the malls)

Use your notebook to add to your list as you learn about essential tools and equipment.

SHOW ONE EMOTION—HAPPY—AND NEVER EVER SWEAR

This is huge because you don't want your sweetface to experience any problems and the way to do that is to be, or at least appear to be, happy all the time. Let's face it, nobody likes anger or sadness as these are negative emotions that need to be banished. So suck it up granny! You want your charismatic cookie to be happy all the time so that's what you need to show him/her. Mellow is another good one to cultivate. When mummy/daddy pick the child up from your house, be cool no matter what. Don't disclose any of the grimy details of your day; for example don't tell them that the mess on the couch kind of irritated you or that your back is killing you because their little lovely is growing beyond your lifting capacity. They may question your suitability as a caregiver.

Curb your bad language because sure as shooting his/her tiny-ness will learn pretty quick to repeat those words at the most embarrassing times. His/her parents will be sure to comment on this practice in spite of the fact that they learned these expletives from you! Remember, it's a whole new world with a different set of expectations.

MAINTAIN YOUR OPTIMUM FITNESS LEVEL

No matter how much we may like to deny that we are old and degenerating, it's important to maintain a façade of good health. So, yeah I used to go to the gym, but now it's totally acceptable to find fitness in other ways.

I say wear high heels as that will give your calves a needed boost. Tone those glutes by doing squats while your teeny practises "up and down". Weights gathering dust in the crawlspace? No worries; press your little pickle into action.

Just find ways to become a buffgramma as this will serve you well for soccer, hockey and other high-impact sports that you will be required to attend. And of course, you'll be standing out in the crowd (See GET WITH THE PROGRAM: BE COMPETITIVE).

NUTRITION AND MEDICAL ISSUES (WITH A NOTE ABOUT POTTY-TRAINING)

Hopefully, your little pickle's mommy will have given up on being his/her only source of food before he/she is popping in at recess for a snack. Soon enough you'll have to consider giving him/her something solid on a spoon. Here's some advice from my experience: "Organic" is basically a cash-grab. All that mushed-up stuff in jars is the same, I figure. Disregard your teeny-weeny's parents when they carry on ad-nauseum about reduce/reuse/recycle and organic. They've been brainwashed by the media. As early as possible introduce baby to the wonderful flavours of processed foods, because that is what he/she will gravitate to soon enough. It's natural. Only childless people shame others for giving their little ones artificial cheese and cotton candy. I'd like to see how they would maintain that kind of self-righteousness with a screamer in tow who wants that goody he saw on TV right now! It's a medical fact that our bodies need starch and sugar.

In case of illness and injury, use your good common sense. All grannies have it. Here's a useful adage when it comes to kids' complaints: If you can't see it, it doesn't exist. Lice, for example, are real; so you need to vigorously scrub that little scalp. Tummy-aches on the other hand could be a figment of an overactive imagination. The only treatment needed for a runny nose is educating your totster. Don't run off to the doc unless you're sure the limb is fractured or the babe is so hot that an egg sizzles on his/her forehead. After all, we're still alive and you can bet that our mothers sorted most things out on their own. Remember that cod-liver oil is good for most ills and poultices can be made from everyday ingredients we all have around the house (now locked up in the cupboard most likely). Doctors' offices and emergency rooms are scary places to be avoided at all costs.

A note about potty-training: I think I speak for most of us when I say that we all got through this. At least for now, we're using grown-up facilities in private and public places and diapers have yet to reappear in our lives. However, some of us experienced long-lasting trauma at the hands of our parents (the details of which I don't choose to get into right now), so don't employ any overt threats in relation to this bodily function. Chill out on this one. Let that little monster determine when and where to become civilized in this regard. If he/she wakes you up at three in the morning with a joyful "I want to sit on my potty", jump up if you can and accommodate his/her wishes. In the transitional stage if your little man wants to pee on the grass, that's okay, because boys are like that; from an early age they seem to like to hang it out in nature.

ALWAYS BE PRESENT

Presence in a physical sense is straightforward. It's taken for granted that you've gotta be there when you're in charge of the welfare of tiny tots. But being present means more than your body on site. It requires a superior level of engagement. Do not stray more than a few inches away. Maintain friendly eye contact and concentrate on the job at hand—immersing yourself in the world of his/her highness. Don't ever let your mind wander to tomorrow's hair appointment and the radical colour in your head. Feel the wind in your unkempt locks as you soar on the swings alongside him/her. Experience the excitement that car-cars provide. Smell the dirt and imagine its delicious flavor. Hear the bow-wow and meow-meow as if for the first time. Touch the snail and revel in it sliminess. See the man in the moon. In other words, involve all of your senses in order to bond with your youngster. It's all about the relationship.

Use your notebook to reflect on ways in which you can enhance your senses which may have become dull with age. Get creative, but stay away from pharmaceuticals.

WATCH TV

Hang on—don't get your knickers in a knot. The truth is, all bambino(a)s need to get a few hours of quality tube time a day. If not, they will be puzzled and overwhelmed when you take them to the toy mega-store. They won't have a clue about those adorable rabbit siblings or the special bond between a giant mouse and a miniature cat. TV is an educational tool that doubles as a darn fine babysitter when you need a break; so crank it up, Granny. TV also serves as the first of many screens in baby's life. You wouldn't want him/her to be without those little hand-held devices that all kids are glued to in restaurants and around the family dinner table, would you? Don't listen to people who proudly proclaim that their offspring do not watch the cursed box. You can tell if they're lying by checking out the cartoon characters on their little one's t-shirt. The odd one will be telling the truth; they're easy to spot—tree-hugger throwbacks to the 60's who haven't evolved with modern times.

IT'S A BOY... OR IS IT A GIRL?

Forget about all that gender stuff. Dress up your little king in a tutu and ballet slippers if you want and adorn your princess with a shaved head and biker chains. Who cares what anybody thinks? You might even go so far as to not disclose the sex (or is it gender?) of your wee biscuit. It's really nobody else's business, after all. It is wise, also, to remain vague when he/she questions you as to whether he/she is a boy or a girl. You might tackle this with something like "What does it really matter, honeypie?" or "Whatever you want to be is fine with gramma, my little sweetness". Don't think past today while you're having fun with this. Your grandchild will have to figure things out for himself/herself in the future, which doesn't concern you. Oh yeah, if your sprout has a name like John or Mary change it so no one will be able to guess the original equipment he/she came with. Look to geography or food groups to confound. "Cedar", "Lake", "Rainstorm", "Avocado", "Multigrain" and "Lettuce" are all fine choices.

Take a few moments to search deep inside yourself for some names that express the personality of your grandness and write them down in your notebook. Remember to think outside the box.

SLEEP

If there was ever a time when you needed more, it's now that your body is on the downturn. But alas, like that sports car, it ain't gonna happen, so get used to it. You might catch a short snooze while TV is in charge, but other than that, when you're at the helm, forget it. Curiously, your little punk also needs to sleep even though he/she may resist. Think about it—if you can induce sleep in the kid you can increase your own down time. I recall my now-deceased aunt slipping my little cousin a bit of codeine or scotch to knock her out, but that's apparently gone by the wayside as an accepted practice. Parents and grandparents need to be creative when it comes to zonking little monkeys out. Breast-feeding is an all-natural sure-fire trick, but don't try it. Aside from the fact that the wells are long-dry, the thought of it is frankly icky. What then? You can walk the floor, rocking and cooing, but that only works for a short period of time. Soon enough your bundle gets quite heavy, quickly catches on to this ploy and asserts his/her disagreement by wriggling out of your weak arms. Note: This is also a safety concern. Consider these options:

- Pretend to sleep but be careful not to actually fall asleep though as this is another safety concern. The hope here is that role-modeling will kick in.

- Drag out those hiking boots and set off for an extended walkabout over hill and dale. If you choose this one, be sure to take along plenty of solid and liquid nourishment for yourself.

- Load your tiny into the car and drive around and around. Be sure to have him/her appropriately attired for sleep. No shoes, jackets (especially those with hoods) or other impediments to keeping him/her sedated when you have to remove him/her from the vehicle. This one is good, but it takes a little practice to shuffle that droopy little soul into the house after your trip. So have the sleeping equipment just inside the door for easy deposit. If you have dogs or other noisy pets, go on ahead and tell them to shut up. While you're there, unplug the phones. I'd put a star beside this one.

- Story-time. The idea behind this is mesmerization. Your soothing voice along with those soft bunny pictures is sure to result in slumber. Just cut to the chase, though. Skip some paragraphs along the way and avoid any stimulating words like "cookie" for example unless you're prepared to start over again.

• If all else fails, go to the mall as this will at least give you an opportunity to check out those stilettos and mini-skirts in spite of the protests of himself/herself who is supposed to be sleeping.

Use your notebook to come up with your own ideas. Don't worry. As time goes on you'll come to a place where you can say "Off you go now. Time for a nap. Nighty-night". But in the meantime, be resourceful! Once again, use as much paper as you like.

TIME

Time will lose all meaning for you. Don't look at the clock. You no longer need the alarm to wake you up because older people who don't have a job to go to just naturally awake before dawn. It's one of the curses of aging. The arrival of your tot will produce greater time-confusion and the sense that it has wings. It will become difficult to remember when he/she was no longer than your arm. Yesterday? Eating, waking and sleeping follow no regular pattern. Cartoons are on TV twenty-four hours a day. This state of mind is not without benefits, however. For example, call someone up at 6:15am because everyone should be awake by then. Or mix yourself a drink while your cherub chomps his/her cheerios. As my mother was fond of saying, "It's noon somewhere", so kick back and get in the zone.

GUNS AND VIOLENCE

Most of us have no difficulty recognizing extreme forms of violence; they involve weapons. I recommend you keep your AK-47s secured in the locked cupboard in your sewing room. That will ensure they are out of reach of chubby little fingers. Some schools of thought propose that "boys will be boys" when it comes to destroying property and limbs. One way to be proactive here is to follow my suggestions regarding gender vagueness (See IT'S A BOY...OR IS IT A GIRL?). That said, never take it for granted that your little missy is beyond causing a whole lot of trouble. Also see SHOW ONE EMOTION—HAPPY—AND NEVER EVER SWEAR. Keep a lid on those negative emotions, because some of them are precursors to violence. Sing and dance but never enquire as to what might be bothering your little hoodster. This could open up a whole can of worms that you just don't need.

THE IMPORTANCE OF KEEPING THEM BUSY

Since it's a given that "idle hands are the devil's work", it is imperative that you keep that smarty-pants on the move. This will serve a myriad of purposes. See CREATE THOSE MEMORIES for example. When I look back on the happy times of my childhood, that bowling trophy springs to mind. Gosh, I wish I could find it now. Also, since you have introduced him/her to the pleasures of processed food (See NUTRITION AND MEDICAL ISSUES), you'll never need those dining chairs again (See SETTING UP THE ENVIRONMENT) because everyone will be quite comfortable with quick stand-up eating during the brief moments between soccer, tai chi and swimming. Activities usually involve other people's kids, so master/miss will learn those valuable life lessons (See LIKE THE ENVIRONMENT BUT ON A DEEPER LEVEL). Similarly, if your junior jock/jockettte shows an inclination for competitive sports, do whatever you can to get him/her to first place. For example, loading him/her up with energy drinks will nicely set the stage for more sophisticated performance enhancing in the future when he/she becomes a professional athlete. A side benefit of all this busy-ness is cudos from the world at large that places a higher value on filling time with organized activities than learning to occupy oneself.

Use your notebook to reflect on all the ways to get that gold ribbon/medal.

MODELING CAREERS AND OTHER LIMELIGHT

Apparently we all have fifteen minutes of fame, but I say shoot for more than that. Start young. Our parents didn't get this, so as a result most of us have only been famous in our minds. But our little duke/duchess can change all that! Hook up with a professional photographer and get a folder going for head shots. It's never too soon to get those glamour photos. It's just hair, makeup and provocative clothing. Get them out there to the world with your new-found internet skills. Somebody's bound to pick them up! It is a must that you find an agent for your star. Go on-line as I'm sure there are lots of guys lining up to mentor little twinkly.

This is important: When you find yourself on a talk show getting beaten up for being a pushy g-parent, make sure your sweetie's got the script down. You wouldn't want anyone to get the impression that he/she did not choose this career at the age of eighteen months—which is what really happened. You might also want to slip the kid a few certificates for botox and other body enhancement procedures for use when he/she comes of age.

DISCIPLINE— IF IT'S EVER REQUIRED

As I have alluded to many times, it's a new world and we grams need to adjust to so many changes it might make your head spin. Earlier I mentioned those phone numbers for kids to nail you (See READ EVERYTHING YOU CAN ABOUT PARENTING SO YOU CAN DO A BETTER JOB THIS TIME AROUND). Just be aware, okay. Some of us grew up getting a cuff upside the head if we neglected to call the old man "sir". As a result, we developed healthy fear, which is akin to respect. Others of us were allowed to pinch our cousins with absolutely no consequences. We developed a cunningness that serves us well in all kinds of situations. I say go for the inbetween if you must employ discipline. Do not, I repeat, do not, get into the "to spank or not to spank" debate. It's a bit like politics and religion which are unwise topics of conversation in my opinion. Anyway we all know that a little whack on the butt never hurt anyone. Just look at all the folks out there who have survived and say they are better for it. You see them in the grocery store smacking red-faced squawkers and telling them to shut-up or else. These people who equate spanking with violence—what's with that? A spank is a learning tool. Some folks say that you should never hit a kid when you're angry. I don't get it. Why would I strike out if I wasn't angry? And forget about "reasoning" with children; it's not possible. We only become reasonable as we age. Enough said; you'll find your own way. As long as no belts or straps are involved you'll do fine.

NOTES TO SELF

Reflect at least monthly on your experience. I suggest you read over the table of contents and review as needed in order to highlight significant progress you are making in each of these areas. Write about your experience. Be honest. This is documentation for you; no one else has to read it unless you invite them to. Just be aware, however, that after you die, the whole thing is up for grabs.

That's it. I'll say goodbye for now. Good luck on your path to granny greatness!

Notes

Notes

Notes

Made in the USA
Charleston, SC
13 May 2014